Old NAIRN

by
Alan Barron

HIGH STREET, NAIRN

An Edwardian photograph taken at the extreme south end of the High Street in an era when someone with a camera was the exception rather than the rule. Isn't it refreshing to see people able to relax and enjoy the full width of the High Street, rather than being crammed on to the pavements on either side.

First published in the United Kingdom, 1999,
by Stenlake Publishing, Ochiltree Sawmill, The Lade,
Ochiltree, Ayrshire, KA18 2NX
Telephone / Fax: 01290 423114

ISBN 1 84033 090 2

ACKNOWLEDGEMENTS

I would like to express my gratitude to the following for their help in providing photographs for reproduction: John M. Semple; Jim Clark; Ian MacPherson; Nairn Fishertown Museum; Alan McGowan, President of Nairn Literary Institute; and Gordon's Sawmill. Thanks are also due to the George Washington Wilson Collection at Aberdeen University Library for permission to reproduce the photographs on pages 9, 11-13, 25-29, 37, 41 and 43, and to the Royal Commission on the Ancient and Historical Monuments of Scotland for permission to use the photograph on page 16. I also wish to thank my cousin David M. Ellen for his assistance with captioning and editing the book.

**This book is dedicated to the memory
of my parents, David and Jean Barron.**

According to George Bain's *History of Nairnshire*, the Old Cross originally stood in the centre of the High Street near the corner of Leopold Street. It was built of stone and lime and needed to be pointed and harled periodically. In 1757 public works carried out by the council included 'removing the old ruinous cross' and 'building a new one'. It is not known exactly when the cross was moved to this location between the Royal Hotel and Ashley House. In the 1960s, when Ashley House was demolished, the cross was moved to its current site beneath the town clock.

INTRODUCTION

Nairn and district has been settled by man since a very early date. There is evidence throughout the vicinity of vitrified forts, stone circles, crannogs (lake dwellings) and cist graves. Flint arrowheads and stone tools have also been found from time to time.

The area formed part of the large and influential kingdom of Moray, ruled by kings or 'mormaers', which at one time stretched from the present Moray area in the east to the shores of the west coast. George Bain's *History of Nairnshire* records that the area was once known as Moreb, then Murief or Moravia, signifying apparently 'the realm by the sea'. The town and its immediate surroundings subsequently evolved to become the County of Nairnshire, third smallest of Scotland's 33 counties.

The area has witnessed the comings and goings of various peoples over the centuries including Stone Age, Iron Age, Bronze Age and Beaker People, (possibly Romans), Picts, Celts, Vikings, Normans, Scots and English.

The town was once known as Invernairn, meaning 'mouth of the river Nairn'. The name Nairn itself is thought to derive from the Gaelic *uisge nearn* – 'water of the alders' – and alders are very prevalent on the banks of the river to this day. It is pronounced 'Nern' and not 'Nairn' as it is commonly called by visitors and other non-Nairnites alike. The town probably grew up as a huddle of dwellings at the top of the High Street Brae around the site of Constabulary Gardens, where the castle of Nairn once stood. This was a wooden structure which was rebuilt in stone by King William the Lion in the twelfth century. The castle was extremely well protected by the river far below, by ditches and ramparts and also by a drawbridge. There was no bridge over the river in those days and the main ford or crossing was down at Brochers Brae beside the present Merryton Bridge (more commonly known as the 'Sewage Bridge'). It was here that Mary, Queen of Scots entered the town on her progress north in 1562.

In years gone by the river alternated between an easterly and a westerly route after it passed the high ground where the road bridge now stands. On its easterly route it flowed through the site of the present Dunbar Golf Course and entered the sea at Kingsteps. When it travelled west it flowed through the links area and joined the sea beside the baths. In the early eighteenth century various attempts were made to direct the path of the river. However it was not until 1820 that work to place the lower reaches in a permanent channel was successfully carried out. This work enabled a breakwater for the protection of boats, based on a design by Thomas Telford, to be built.

The Moray floods of 1829 caused havoc in the area, however, and totally wrecked the harbour, which had to be reconstructed. The main development of the Fishertown dates from around this time and helped to attract fishermen from the outlying villages of Delnies to the west and Maviston to the east. These fishermen brought their families into the town and took up feus to erect houses in Park Street and Society Street. Society Street was named after the Fishermen's Society which was founded in 1797 to look after the interests of the fishing community. This was one of the first friendly societies to be founded in the country, and provided sterling service during an era when life was very hard and expectations were few. The society owned a mort cloth or shroud which was rented out to families burying loved ones. The income generated from this was distributed to the needy.

By virtue of the limited occupations available within the town, Nairnites have spread themselves far and wide over the years. Indeed descendants of Nairn folk can be found in virtually every English-speaking country in the world. In the days of the Empire a number found employment with the army and navy, and several, including General Sir Herbert MacPherson, Colonel James Augustus Grant of the Nile, Lieutenant-General William R. Gordon, and Captain James Rose, Royal Navy, went on to have very distinguished careers. The town and county has never been slow to respond to the needs of the nation, and many of its sons and daughters laid down their lives not only in the two great wars of the twentieth century, but also in various other smaller wars and skirmishes over the centuries.

Many centuries ago there were two distinct communities living in Nairn. People on the landward side of the town spoke mainly Gaelic, while the fisherfolk spoke Scots or English. King James the first and sixth must have been aware of this, because it is on record that he boasted to his court not long after taking up the English throne that he had a town in Scotland, so long, that the inhabitants at one end did not understand the language spoken by those at the other. It is said that the Highland line crosses through Nairn. Certainly so far as accents are concerned, Nairnites speak with a soft Highland tongue, more akin to the natives of Inverness, whilst only a few miles east the accent starts to become quite broad.

Nairnshire has a genteel beauty, nestling as it does between the Monadliadh Mountains and the southern shores of the Moray Firth and occupying part of that fertile strip of land known as the 'Laich O' Moray'. Because of its sheltered location the area generally benefits from a lower level of rainfall than most parts of Scotland, as well as less severe winter conditions.

The main occupations in the area around the turn of the century, the period principally covered by this book, were farming and fishing, both of which were very labour-intensive. In 1860 Nairn's fishing industry boasted 105 boats and 410 fishermen; the recorded burgh population in 1861 was 3,835. Much of the landward area was and still is in the ownership of a few families, the Earls of Cawdor, the Roses of Kilravock, the Brodies of Brodie, the Brodies of Lethen and the Earls of Leven & Melville. The Dunbars of Boath, once a very influential family to the immediate east of the town and through whose benevolence the Dunbar Golf Course owes its existence, no longer live in the area.

Nairn's halcyon days as a holiday resort covered the years 1895 to 1965, since when the town has had to compete with foreign package holidays. During more recent years a number of bad summers, combined with a very strong pound, have encouraged even more Britons to journey abroad and also discouraged foreign visitors from coming to Scotland. The town's major attributes – friendly people, beautiful beaches and marvellous golf courses – are still very much with us, and will, I am sure, prove their worth in attracting visitors in the future. Nairn remains one of the finest places in the country in which to live, bring up a family and grow old.

The first bridge over the river on this site was erected by William Rose of Clava in 1631. He was provost of the town at the time and funded the building work himself. The bridge was described as 'a magnificent structure, of many arches, with a splendid high pillared gateway, richly carved and ornamented'. No traces of that bridge now remain. In 1829 the famous Moray Floods carried away a large part of a later bridge, built in 1803. The bridge in the picture dates from 1868 when partial re-erection works were carried out. In 1936 it was widened and strengthened, and a walk below the eastmost arch shows that its width was doubled. The old and new structures can be clearly seen, and a close examination of the old arch from this viewpoint reveals numerous masons' marks chiselled into the stone blocks.

In 1858 the Inverness and Aberdeen Junction Railway company built a line to connect Nairn with Keith, thereby creating a continuous rail link between Inverness and Aberdeen. Part of the work involved the erection of this four-spanned viaduct over the River Nairn which has been the subject of so many postcards over the years. The coming of the railway brought increased prosperity to Nairn and its main expansion as a holiday resort can be traced to this time. Fishwives took advantage of the railway, using it to transport their fresh and smoked fish to Inverness to sell. Cricket is believed to have been introduced to Nairn by Englishmen building the railway line from Inverness to the town.

This picture was taken in January 1895 during one of the most severe winters ever experienced in Nairn. The 'big freeze' lasted fully two months and must have caused a great deal of hardship and discomfort to the townsfolk in the days before central heating or double glazing.

Taken in 1860, this is the earliest known photograph of Nairn High Street and shows the old clock tower, which was replaced in 1870. The three-storey building in the centre of the picture was a town house belonging to the Roses of Kilravock. Most of the wealthy county families had town houses, which provided a home-from-home for longer stays and avoided the need to undertake uncomfortable coach rides twice in a day on shorter visits. The Duke of Cumberland lodged in this house on the night before the battle of Culloden, which also happened to be his 25th birthday. Whilst he slumbered in relative comfort, his troops were billeted just outside the town at Balblair, although their discomfort was alleviated by extra grog rations granted by the duke to celebrate his birthday.

The building in the middle of the picture was formerly occupied by Simpson the grocer. Shortly after this photograph was taken in the early 1960s, it was purchased and fitted out by Heard's the Ironmongers, to become arguably the largest shop of its kind in Scotland. The shop on the right, formerly Boyne & Martin, plumbers, and now a restaurant, is one of the last surviving buildings on the High Street built with its gable end onto the street. The building on the left, occupied by Woolworths, stands on the site of the old Secession Church which had previously been located near the foot of Castle Lane.

The Highland Hotel, photographed in the 1940s before Dr Grigor's statue was moved to its present site outside Viewfield House. Like the Royal Marine, the Highland Hotel tried hard to survive as holiday habits changed over the past twenty years, but was ultimately forced to close. The building is currently undergoing a metamorphosis and will soon emerge from behind its cover of scaffolding having been converted into flats. The hotel annexe, just visible on the right behind the garage, was demolished a few years ago and replaced by housing.

Looking north along the High Street c.1885. The post office is the building on the left with a lantern above the entrance, and a postman standing outside. It later moved to the premises now occupied by Messrs C. G. Higgins & Co. The small thatched cottage on the right belonged to a Mrs Orr and was pulled down at the turn of the century; the building which replaced it is now occupied by Burnett & Forbes, outfitters. Further down the street on the left, trees can be seen outside the former National Bank (now the Royal Bank of Scotland), known to generations of Nairnites as 'Lamb's Bank' after the solicitor/agent who prosecuted his business there in the late 1800s. Still further down the street a tree belonging to 'Ashley', the home of the Asher family, overhangs the street. The tree was removed in the 1960s when Ashley was demolished and replaced by the flat-roofed library building and car park behind. The picture predates the Highland Hotel and Doctor Grigor's statue.

A lively but unhurried picture of the High Street, taken in the early 1930s, when even the police had time to stand in the road chatting. The photograph may have been taken on a Thursday as the group of men on the left beside the lamp-post look very much like farmers, and it was their custom to gather at this spot on market days long after markets ceased to be held in the town.

The solitary figure of a boy lends the only animation to this photograph looking south-west along the High Street *circa* 1895. Close inspection reveals that Mrs Orr's house (see page 9) has had guttering and a down-pipe installed, and some thatching has been replaced by slates to enable the water to enter the gutter. Doctor Grigor's statue was erected on 31 May 1890 by a very grateful town in recognition of the many benevolent acts undertaken by the doctor over a period of forty years spent amongst Nairn folk. It was moved to its present position outside Viewfield House in 1950 because of the increasing volume of traffic. Recent talk of moving the statue back to a site adjacent to the Royal Bank has been put on hold for the time being. The Highland Hotel, originally known as the Station Hotel, was built on the site of the walled garden. In view of the unmade roads, the line of granite setts joining the pavements must have been a godsend during inclement weather, especially for the women with their long flowing dresses.

This view of the High Street dates from after 1870, when the present clock tower was erected, but before 1877, when the Waverley Hotel was built. The building on the left was subsequently removed to provide an entrance to Constabulary Gardens and House from the High Street. Before that the entrance was via Castle Lane. The picture was taken by George Washington Wilson, the famous Aberdeen photographer, or one of his many employees. Wilson's collection of 40,000 glass plate negatives, which includes 68 of Nairn and Nairnshire, is held by Aberdeen University Library.

A comparison of this picture with the one opposite shows major improvements to the road and pavements. The High Street entrance to Constabulary Gardens, with its handsome pillars, has been created. The pillars still stand although they have since been moved further back from the edge of the pavement. Prior to its demolition in the 1960s, the first building beyond the pillars with its gable end to the street was occupied by Mr MacRae the travel agent. The building on the right, just beyond the town clock, dated from 1668 but was rebuilt in 1902 and is now occupied by the Caledonian Hotel. The Waverley Hotel stands further along the street on the right.

The Harbour, Nairn

Before the Drifter Basin was built in 1932, boats moored all the way up the river channel as far as the gas works. The intake to the left, known as the 'maggot', was high and dry at low tide and was an ideal place for boats to be painted or repaired and then refloated when required. Many boats which were past their days of useful service were abandoned and left to rot at the maggot.

Looking up river *circa* 1895. The large building to the left is the Episcopal Church or Church of England Chapel which was opened in 1845 on the corner between the Forres Road and Lochloy Road. The congregation was continually at loggerheads with the members of the Scottish Episcopal Church concerning their position and standing. After Rev. Dr Edwin Wrenford left in 1879, services were discontinued. The church subsequently lay derelict for many years before being dismantled, stone by stone, and transported by sailing ship to Lochinver where it was re-erected and is still being used as a place of worship to this day. For many years the minister of the church at Lochinver was a Nairn man, Rev. Freddie Hurst.

Nairn Harbour *circa* 1890 with the trading barque *Bella* of Findhorn in the foreground. The lifeboat shed can be seen through the ship's rigging. The vessels in the background are Zulus, so-called because they were invented at the time of the Zulu wars in Africa. These were very common around the inner Moray Firth area from 1879 up until the First World War, and combined the best features of Scaffie and Fifie type boats, with the former's steeply raked stern and the latter's vertical bow. The Zulu has been described by more than one writer as the most noble sailing craft ever designed in these islands.

The large Zulu, *Look Sharper* INS 2159, belonged to John and Alec Hogg and John Main Bochel. Hogg and Main were both common family names in the Fishertown. The surname Main is thought to derive from the Norse 'Magnus'. At one time it was so widespread that teenames or bynames had to be used to differentiate one family of Mains from another. By the latter years of the nineteenth century there were no fewer than 32 teenames being used, including Baillie, Bunker, Callie, Coggs, Captain, Coup or Cope, Downie, Duggie, Ellen, Hastings, Ian, McIntosh, Mein, Sergeant and Wallace. The name Ralph was another common surname and is thought to come from the Norse 'Hrolf'. Other names which were once very prevalent in the Fishertown were Barron, Finlayson, Jamieson, Storm and Wilson.

A typical Nairn Zulu, *Hackilah* INS 561, heading out to sea past the east pier, which is in a ruinous condition. The *Hackilah* was owned by John Fraser of 10 Burntisland Street and William Barron of 1 Union Street. There are women aboard on this occasion (which due to superstition was very unusual) along with some well-dressed men, which suggests that the vessel might be undergoing sea trials. The powerful steam capstan which can be seen astern was used to raise the huge lug-sail. The boat would have had dark brown sails and been painted black with a white water line. It is fully decked and would have been able to travel to East Anglia and such places in search of the 'silver darlings'. Provisions for such a trip would be obtained from Hugh Wilson, David Bunker or Alec Wallace, all ship chandlers in the Fishertown.

A photograph commemorating the launch of Nairn's first lifeboat on 9 March 1878. Having arrived by train she was 'drawn from the railway station by four horses and a large body of men hauling on ropes'. Lady Dunbar of Boath named the boat *The Caulfield and Ann*. After launching, the crew, wearing cork life jackets and red caps, rowed out some distance before returning by sail. The coxswain was Alexander Storm and the bowman was William Main Cope. The lifeboat station was closed in 1911 and the lifeboat transferred to Cromarty.

This photograph was taken outside 'Allasdale' in St Ninian Road during the Nairn Harbour campaign of 1928-1929. It was not until 1932, however, that the Drifter Basin or harbour as we know it today was opened. The gentleman on the cart wearing the top hat is Geordie Patience, a worthy of non-existent means who was well-liked by the townsfolk. Standing to the right wearing a black hat and coat is Councillor Duggie, who fought tirelessly for the new harbour.

Nairn Harbour, or Drifter Basin as it was sometimes called, photographed *c*.1935, just three years after being built. The steam drifters were roughly 80 to 90 feet long and generally each employed 10 men. Young boys would start their sea careers at the age of 14, working as cooks on board the drifters on a set wage, and hopefully working their way up to become boat-owners in due course. The drifters followed herring around the coast of Britain and in due season Nairn boats could be found at Shetland, Ireland and East Anglia. This meant that their crews were away from home for considerable periods of time, and it was left to the womenfolk to run the homes and bring up often large families on their own during the men's absence. By the time the harbour was built, the fishing industry in Nairn was in a terminal decline. Many of the steam drifters were sold for scrap during the 1930s and at the time it was very common for fathers to forbid their sons from taking up a fishing career. My grandfather's drifter *Holmerose* INS 372 was sold for £20. My father kept the lifeboat and sold it for more than the scrap value of the drifter after the 1939-45 war.

Right: Ann Main McIntosh was born in 1835 and married John Barron in October 1860. She was known affectionately as 'Big Gran' because of her size and height. When her husband and sons were engaged in the inshore fishing it was her responsibility to run the household, obtain bait for further fishing trips, help bait the lines of hooks and – especially – to sell the fish. It was common for fishwives to walk for many, many miles in order to call on their regular country customers. Quite often they would barter fish for vegetables and dairy products, which would be transported home in the fish creels. Big Gran was the 'Chancellor of the Exchequer', with total control of all the family finances. In later years when her husband and sons travelled further afield in search of the herring shoals in the larger-decked boats, they would hand her all their hard-earned money on returning to Nairn. When her sons John and Alexander were married in the 1890s they were both given £20 to start their married lives.

Above: John Main McIntosh, otherwise known as 'Jocky Breekie', was my great-grandmother's brother. Because of his photogenic appearance a number of different photographs of him have survived, and this one is captioned 'An Old Salt at Nairn'. In his day, the fishing community was very superstitious and avoided saying certain words like 'salmon' or 'Ross' lest ill fortune befall them. The men avoided meeting a minister when proceeding to their boats, and if they did so would turn round and go back home and start their journey again. When leaving harbour they would turn the bows of their boats in the direction of the sun, as to turn against it was considered to be very unlucky. If they unintentionally muttered any forbidden words while on board they would grab something made of iron and shout 'cauld iron'. Whistling whilst at sea was strictly forbidden in case it summoned up gales. Despite their superstitious ways, the fisherfolk were a God-fearing community.

A fairly uncommon view looking down Harbour Street from just outside Asher's shop at the corner of the High Street Brae and Bridge Street. A sizeable group of Nairn 'loonies' has gathered to animate the picture. All the buildings in the left and right foreground were removed as part of the bridge widening works in the 1930s. The cart is situated outside the Harbour Street Post Office, which is now owned by the author. Diagonally opposite, beyond the group of boys, is Hugh Barron the plumber and tinsmith's shop, with samples of his many wares hanging outside. Harbour Street was the gateway to the Fishertown area, where the seafaring population lived apart from its 'uptown' neighbours.

Central Beach looking west. Considering the huge expanse of sand which lay to the east of the harbour it may be wondered why the stony Central Beach was favoured by visitors and townsfolk. The reason was the lack of a bridge across the river to where the caravan site is now. The nearest one was the Merryton Bridge (the 'Sewage Bridge'), which meant a long walk for visitors wishing to enjoy a swim in the sea. In 1895 tickets for the bathing machines could be obtained from the refreshment stall or Wm. Dallas, chemist at 37 High Street. Tickets cost 4d for one coach or 6d for two or three coaches.

Looking west along Central Beach *circa* 1890, with the Royal Marine Hotel standing sentinel on the links. The hotel was built in 1860, and owed its existence to the foresight and planning of Doctor Grigor, who was quick to realise Nairn's potential as a holiday resort. The building on the ridge to the right of the hotel is The Clifton Hotel, formerly known as Clifton House, which was built and run as a guest house by Provost Leslie and his wife. This picture was taken prior to the erection of the bandstand, which didn't appear on the links until July 1884.

Looking east towards the harbour *c*.1885. A number of Scaffies, which look as though they have been left to rot, are lying on the beach above the high water mark. These predated the more popular Zulu and were distinguished by their canoe bow and raked stern. They were either undecked or only half-decked and were unsuitable for long fishing trips. In the early days, before properly established harbours and waterproofed clothing and footwear, it was very common at Nairn and other fishing ports for the womenfolk to carry the men out to the boats on their backs to ensure that they started their trip dry. The Royal Marine Hotel stands on Quarry Road, subsequently given the more genteel name of Marine Road. The edge of the quarry can be seen on the extreme left of the picture. It provided stone for the construction of the hotel but has since been filled in, and the putting green now occupies the site.

Looking east along the Bathing Beach at the turn of the twentieth century, with a Zulu drying its mainsail in the old harbour. A closer look at the spit of land in the far distance reveals the Culbin Sands before afforestation work commenced. Until the early years of the twentieth century the area resembled a desert and was prone to shift with the force of the wind. A proper promenade overlooking the beach was subsequently built between the swimming pool and the harbour. This provided an attractive feature for holidaymakers and also offered the Fishertown some protection from the sea. Parts of the Fishertown are below sea-level and very high tides had been known to swamp the 'Parkie' and parts of Park Street in days gone by. The salmon nets, which were brought out at the beginning of the season in February each year, are now a thing of the past.

Two ladies enjoying a seat and a blether overlooking the Firth. The building to the right is 'The Grigor Shelter', which still retains some of its rounded slates. The site where the shelter was built was the subject of an acrimonious dispute in the 1860s. Lieut. Colonel Findlay of Millbank had formed an artillery corps to protect the town against any possibility of French invasion from the sea, and had begun preparing the site for a gun battery. Unknown to the Findlay camp, however, Dr Grigor and a number of supporters had gone to law to obtain an interdict to prevent the creation of the battery on that particular site. They felt that it was too near the Marine Hotel and feared that the noise of guns being fired would annoy the guests. Brodie of Brodie was eventually asked to find a diplomatic solution to the problem and, in due course, an alternative site for the gun battery was found near the harbour.

THE BATHING BEACH, NAIRN. 3973. G.W.W.

SALT WATER SWIMMING-BATHS, NAIRN.

3960. G.W.W.

The Nairn Salt Water Swimming Baths were opened on Saturday 28 June 1873 on the site of the present swimming pool. The baths were built from stone excavated from the surrounding area and the building laid down on the bedrock which can be seen stretching out to sea nearby. Dr Grigor was the leading light in getting the enterprise off the ground. The fountain in the centre of the pool was used to pump 360 gallons of fresh sea water per minute into the baths, with excess water escaping back to the sea via an overflow pipe. The immense quantity of glass used in the construction of the roof ensured that the baths were very bright and airy. The reflections in the picture certainly enhance the view substantially.

CHILDRENS PLAYGROUND AT THE BEACH, NAIRN

D 436

A scene close to the hearts of generations of children, showing the beach, playground and paddling pool. Over £30,000 was spent only recently installing a pumping station to supply clean water for the paddling pool. Despite that there were plans to close the pool in 1999 because European Union bureaucracy dictated that the water quality was still below acceptable levels. However, following a huge petition, which was eagerly signed by locals and holiday-makers of all ages, further work was carried out to enable the pool to remain open.

ON THE BEACH, NAIRN.

218541

A bevy of bathing beauties photographed on the Central Beach *circa* 1930. The groynes in the background were erected at no small cost to help build up the level of the beach. The exercise was so successful that they have now been almost completely buried by sand.

No book about Nairn would be complete without mentioning golf, that most satisfying yet frustrating of games. There are two major courses in the town, belonging to the Nairn Golf Club and the Nairn Dunbar Golf Club, known to most locals as the 'West' and the 'Dunbar'. They were founded in 1887 and 1899 respectively. There is little doubt that the excellent golfing facilities in the town played an important part in attracting both visitors and permanent settlers at the turn of the century.

The caravan site has been an integral part of Nairn and its tourist facilities since 1958. The site was established on rough ground on the east side of the river opposite the harbour. The town council initially operated it, but leased it out in the 1960s, since when it has changed hands a few times but has been continually improved. In the earlier days living conditions on the site were rather cramped, particularly during the Glasgow Fair fortnight, when Nairn's population almost doubled. In those days water had to be carried to the caravans from central taps on site and gas was the only form of lighting. Toilet facilities were a bit limited and it was not unheard of for people to queue at busy times. Nowadays of course, running water, electricity, showers and television sets are the order of the day.

A photograph of the 1913 Nairn Show, held in Seabank Road. William Whitelaw of Monkland House was president of the Nairnshire Farming Society at the time. Before houses were built on it, this field stretched down towards the sea on the same side of the road as the Parish Church. The Nairnshire Farming Society, which holds the shows, was founded in 1798 to promote agricultural improvements in the county. The present showground, The Farmers' Field, was acquired from Viscount Finlay, who owned Newton House, for £1,000 in 1928. In recent years it has proved to be too small for the society's purposes, and its members have been looking at a plan to relocate to a new ground. Despite the vicissitudes in farming over the past few years the society is still flourishing. Indeed it could be argued that the existence of such an organisation has never been more important.

A photograph of Nairn Games Day dating from the late 1920s or early 1930s, when folk came from far and wide and large crowds were an annual feature. Some even travelled across the firth by steamer from Cromarty in the days when the *Ailsa* sailed these waters. The crowd of people in the foreground look as though they are dressed in their Sunday best clothes. As they do now, most exiled Nairnites would coincide a return visit to the town with the games and would be sure to bump into fellow exiles and other 'weel kent' faces. It was also quite common for Nairn fishermen working out of the west coast to tie up their boats on the games weekend and take a train back home in time for the event. Traditionally the games have always been held on the first Saturday after 12 August (the 'Glorious Twelfth'). This date was chosen to accommodate the arrival of shooting parties who took houses in the town at the beginning of the shooting season. The games were held on a different date for the first time in 1999. It is a common belief in Nairn that once the games have passed we can look forward to the onset of winter.

GAMES DAY ON THE LINKS, NAIRN

800

River Nairn and Jubilee Bridge.

The Jubilee Bridge was opened in 1887 to celebrate fifty years of Queen Victoria's reign. The wood for the bridge was gifted by Earl Cawdor and Lady Gordon Cathcart of Kinsteary, and the pillars were painted and varnished by the apprentice painters of the town as their contribution. A flood in 1915 swept the bridge away, following which a similar one was built. This too was destroyed by a flood. The present concrete bridge was built on the same site as its two predecessors. In the background is the Glencawdor Distillery, which ceased production in the 1920s. The stonework from the demolished distillery was used to build the houses at Broadhill, and the only reminder of its existence is the Glencawdor Cottages, which are still occupied adjacent to the distillery site today.

The Old Parish Church at the foot of Church Street on the west bank of the river. A number of church buildings have stood on this site since soon after the Reformation. Prior to that the church of Nairn stood on what is now the site of Constabulary Gardens. The building in this photograph dated from 1810 and incorporated part of the walls and foundations of the previous church. By the late 1880s various faults in the building were being reported and dry rot was discovered. A decision was eventually made to erect a new church elsewhere, after which the old building was abandoned and quickly fell into disrepair.

A packed public hall photographed in August 1923 at the start of the Nairn United Free High Church bazaar. The bazaar was held over a two day period and was opened by Brodie of Brodie DSO, Lord Lieutenant, on the Thursday, and Provost Kenneth MacRae on the Friday. It was organised to raise funds for the purchase of a manse and an organ. In all £1,920 was raised, a huge sum at the time, bearing in mind that it cost Nairn fishermen about the same amount to purchase a 70 to 90 foot steam drifter. By comparison, shortly after the bazaar was held the *Nairnshire Telegraph* carried an advertisement for a sale by public roup of 18 Simpson Street, consisting of a kitchen, parlour, 3 bedrooms, yard with 3-stalled stable and cart shed. The upset price was £230.

A sea of faces assembled on a cold winter's day in January 1901 to hear the accession of King Edward VII proclaimed following the death of Queen Victoria. In the days before television and other domestic distractions, public events were very well attended and, fortunately, many were recorded on camera. Copies of photographs of this event were available in various sizes from W. G. Sprunt, The Studio, Queen Street. Participants including the police, trumpeters, town band, guard of honour, sheriff, provost, Lord Lieutenant and many others gathered at the drill hall and then proceeded up King Street, along Leopold Street and down the High Street to the market cross in front of the Old Parish Church manse. This was the traditional site of royal proclamations, and the ceremony was held there amid a fierce snowstorm.

Looking north-east along Academy Street from the tower of the Parish Church. St Mary's Catholic Church, in the foreground, was erected in 1864 to meet the religious needs of a fairly large number of Gaelic-speaking crofters who settled in Nairn having been evicted from the island of Barra in the 1850s. The large building in the middle distance is the academy, or Roses Academical Institution as it was known until the 1950s. The house to its right is Ivybank House which, along with the adjoining gardens, made way for the academy's expansion. The academy has of course been resident at its new location in Duncan Drive since the 1970s, and the old building is now Rosebank Primary School.

Looking west along a very leafy Academy Street in the 1930s. A group of message boys has stopped in the middle of the road for a 'news'. The picture is striking because of the complete absence of motors vehicles and apparent lack of expectation of any. When the right-hand side of the street was widened in the early 1960s 'Glenridding', the house in the foreground, was demolished.

Looking along Leopold Street towards Academy Street. Leopold Street was formerly known as Pole Road because of a sign which stood in it pointing the way to Inverness. The wall on the right was subsequently removed to make way for the Regal Cinema development, which in the late 1950s incorporated a popular roller-skating rink. The *Nairnshire Telegraph* office, on the left, is run by the Bain family.

King Street looking north prior to road widening works carried out in 1962/63. The Congregational Church manse, part of which can be seen on the left, was demolished, as were the buildings just beyond the Free Church. The yard on the right belonged to Colin Young the builder, and is now the site of a block of flats appropriately called Colin Young Place. The Free Church stands on a bog, and the unfortunate gentleman who won the contract to build it in 1909 went bankrupt owing to the difficulties he experienced in trying to erect the building on solid foundations. Because of these problems, plans to build the church manse at the same time had to be put on hold until a later date.

This unusual view was taken from a window at the back of Barron House, formerly the Bank of Scotland and before that the British Linen Bank. Prior to that the site was occupied by Anderson's Hotel. The view looks down the side of Gordon Street before the Free Church had been built in the right foreground. The garden area in the middle was subsequently occupied by Mrs Tolmie's house, 'Kogarah', and Colin Young & Son's builders yard. The Congregational Church manse and garden can be seen at the right-hand edge of the picture. They were swept away in the 1960s to allow the Back Road (King Street) to be widened. The Havelock Hotel nestles just beyond the church and has still to receive its Victorian metal canopy. It was built in 1857 and was originally owned by His Excellency The Emir of Jaipur. It was used as the Emir's summer residence in 1857 whilst he was in exile during the Sepoy Mutiny, and was named by him after Major General Sir Henry Havelock, hero of the relief of Lucknow, who at that time was the only Englishman ever to have led a Scottish Regiment.

The foundation stone for the new Parish Church was laid on 29 August 1894. J. A. Grant of Household officiated at the ceremony along with Rev. James Burns, the appointed minister. The church was built at the corner of Seabank Road and Academy Street on farmland donated by Colonel Clarke of Achareidh.

A commemorative photograph taken as the Parish Church neared completion. The blocks of stone sticking out above the builders' heads on either side of the doorway were carved into the flying angels which can be seen today. Building work was completed in July 1897.

Monkland House, situated beside the swimming baths and commanding a magnificent view over the Moray Firth, was built and occupied by the Whitelaw family. The best known member of the family must be the recently deceased Lord William (Willie) Whitelaw, former Conservative MP, whose posts during his career included Secretary of State for Northern Ireland, Leader of the House of Commons and Lords, and Deputy Prime Minister. His mother, Winifred, who lived in this area for many years, was a formidable force in local politics. Monkland House was sold by the Whitelaws many years ago, and was badly damaged by fire in the early 1960s.

Built in 1460, Kilravock Castle (pronounced Kilrock) is the ancestral home of the Roses of Kilravock, a family of Norman descent which settled in these parts in the thirteenth century and is first mentioned at Geddes in 1230. In 1293 Hugh Rose of Geddes, having married Marjory Bisset of Kilravock, obtained a charter to the Kilravock lands from the king, and Roses have lived there from that day to this. The burial ground of the Roses continues to be at Geddes churchyard where there is a family enclosure. The castle and estate is one of very few in the country which has been continually inhabited by the same family through unbroken succession over so many centuries. The present Chief of Clan Rose, Miss Elizabeth Rose of Kilravock, has given over the castle as a Christian guest house.

Boath House was the country seat of the Dunbars of Boath, descendants of David Dunbar, Dean of Moray. He died in 1556 and was buried in the kirkyard at Auldearn. The family's lands were situated to the east of Nairn and included, at one time, Merryton, Broadhill, Boathpark, Achnacloich, Camperdown, Balmakeith and various portions around Auldearn. At one time a townhouse belonging to the Dunbars was located at the west corner of Bridge Street. The present Boath House was built by Sir James Dunbar, who was knighted in 1810 and created a baronet in 1814. His grandson, Sir Alexander Dunbar, donated land to help create the Nairn Dunbar Golf Course which was opened in 1899. Tragically, Sir Alexander drowned in the River Nairn a year later, and the estate and title passed to his brother Frederick who disposed of the property.

Cawdor Castle, in its present form, is arguably one of the most beautiful structures of its kind in Scotland. Permission to erect the original three-storey tower or keep was granted by King James II in 1454 to his erstwhile personal attendant, Thane William VI of Calder, who held the title from 1442 to 1468. The various alterations and additions which have been made over the centuries have served to enhance the overall beauty of the structure. Tradition has it that the castle was erected around a hawthorn tree after Thane William was told in a dream to load his treasure chest onto an ass and to build his keep wherever the beast came to a standstill. Whether this is true or not there are the remains of a tree in the dungeon, and when these were carbon-dated a few years ago they were said to be approximately 600 years old, tallying with the date the keep was built. The castle and estate was known as Calder after the original owners. In 1510 Muriel Calder, heiress to the property, married Sir John Campbell in Argyllshire and in 1524 she and her husband came north to settle permanently in Nairnshire. The title appears to have changed from Calder to Cawdor following Shakespeare's misspelling of the name in his play *Macbeth*.